FOR THE GREATEST COOK WHO HAS IT ALL!

A Funny Book About Cooking

Bruce Miller and Team Golfwell

This is book number 19 in our *For People Who Have Everything Series.*

Cover by Queen Graphics. All images are from Creative Commons or Shutterstock

ISBN 9798859196975 KDP Paperback b&w interior

Looking good. "There is no spectacle on earth more appealing than that of a man or woman in the act of cooking dinner for those they love."

-- Thomas Wolfe

Kitchen truisms. "No woman ever shot a man while he was washing the dishes."

- "Table manners are for people that aren't hungry."

- "The only reason I have a kitchen is because it came with the house!"

- "The perfect food would taste as good as fresh popcorn smells."

- "This kitchen would be clean if only people would stop eating here."

- "Clean the kitchen not because you want to, but because if you don't Mom will lose her sh#t."

- "It doesn't matter how expensive your kitchen is if you are a bad cook."

- "A guy who knows how to cook is really handsome."

- "If we're not meant to have midnight snacks, why is there a light in the fridge?"

- "When life gives you lemons, throw them away and get some bacon."

- "You can't buy happiness, but you can buy cupcakes, and that's kind of the same thing."

Outdoor cooking. "My first outdoor cooking memories are full of erratic British summers, Dad swearing at a barbecue that he couldn't put together, and eventually eating charred sausages, feeling brilliant."

-- Jamie Oliver

Who started to call it BBQ? Spanish explorer Gonzalo Fernández De Oviedo y Valdés (commonly known as Oviedo) supposedly was the first to use the word "barbecoa" in print in Spain in 1526. [1] He used it in his book, "Diccionario de la Lengua Española (2nd Edition) of the Real Academia Española".

Further on in this book, there is more discussion of the origins of Barbecue, a word that brings excitement to many avid eaters who love grilled food!

After Columbus landed in the Americas in 1492, the Spaniards found the Taíno people roasting meat over a grill consisting of a wooden framework resting on sticks above a fire. The flames and smoke rose and enveloped the meat, giving it a certain flavor that we all love today. [2]

Oviedo was the first European (Spaniard) to arrive at the islands in 1492.

The Taíno are the indigenous people of the Caribbean in the islands that are now known as Cuba, the Dominican Republic, Jamaica, Haiti, Puerto Rico, the Bahamas, and the northern

Lesser Antilles. [3] The Taino were also the first New World people encountered by Columbus in the Bahamas on October 12, 1492. [4]

If you ever visit the Caribbean, say thanks to a Taino descendant for showing Oviedo how to barbecue Caribbean style!

Exhausting. "It can be exhausting eating a meal cooked by a man.

"With a woman, it's, 'Ho hum, pass the beans'. A guy, you have to act like he just built the Taj Mahal."

— Deb Caletti, The Queen of Everything

Caring. "Cooking is a caring and nurturing act. It's kind of the ultimate gift for the family."

-- Curtis Stone, Celebrity Chef

True story. A man was waiting in the customer service/refunds line at a local department store. There was a lady in front of him returning a disposable barbecue telling the service lady she wanted a refund since there was no meat in the barbecue.

The service person politely explained it is a disposable barbecue and it just cooks the meat and doesn't include meat or any food with it.

The lady became very embarrassed and began to walk away when the service person said, "This receipt shows you bought three of these. Do you want to return the other two also?"

She replied as she walked away, "I can't since I've got them at home in the freezer."

Cutting the pizza. "You better cut the pizza in four pieces because I'm not hungry enough to eat six.

    -- Yogi Berra

Cookies. "When I buy cookies, I eat just four and throw the rest away. But first I spray them with Raid, so I won't dig them out of the garbage later.

"Be careful, though, because Raid really doesn't taste that bad."

    -- Janette Barber, Comedian, TV Producer, and writer.

Does cooking food make us smarter? According to Professor Richard Wrangham of Harvard University, when man started to cook food over fire, the eating of cooked meat speeded up our evolution. [5] In his book, "Catching Fire: How Cooking Made Us Human" he has found "that the ability to harness fire and cook food allowed the brain to grow and the digestive tract to shrink, giving rise to our ancestor Homo erectus some 1.8 million years ago." [6] He also says at that time there is evidence man started to cook food over fire.

He points out animals don't cook food. "Cooking is the signature feature of the human diet, and indeed, of human life…. It's the development that underpins many other changes that have made humans so distinct from other species."

Also, "Cooking is what makes the human diet 'human,' and the most logical explanation for the advances in brain and body size over our ape ancestors," Wrangham says. "It's hard to imagine the leap to Homo erectus without cooking's nutritional benefits." [7]

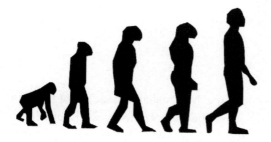

It's easy to make dinner...

"I didn't feel like cooking tonight, so I made a sandwich for dinner.

"It wasn't so much as a sandwich as it was just bread...I guess more just grain.

"Fermented grain...Distilled, fermented grain.

"I had whisky for dinner tonight."

     -- Anon.

Loving food. "Never trust a skinny cook."

-- Iain Hewitson, Australian celebrity chef.

A simple mistake. **True story**. My husband made pizza for the first time, and he knew many cheeses extremely well but when we tasted the pizza, it tasted strange. We all thought the pizza would be one of the best with many different cheese flavors. It tasted strangely sweet.

No one in the family said anything about it until he served himself a slice and took a bite and gave us a strange look.

Turns out, he added powdered sugar, instead of flour, to the dough! The dough was tough and flat and sickeningly sweet.

We all had a good laugh including my husband who laughed the loudest!

What is it? Remove the outside, then cook the inside, then eat the outside, then throw away the inside. What is it?

Answer p. 99

Showing your love. More research has shown that preparing food for the family or others and sharing food has a strong, bonding role in many cultures. [8] At celebrations, birthdays, etc., food is a feature of those events (besides the featured person or event).

It's been found cooking is a way to give back to others just as much as it's a way to give love to ourselves and others. [9]

If your kids don't like milk. Try lemon-lime soda and milk. Sound crazy? Pour cold milk and cold lemon-lime soda and pour equal parts into a glass.

Sounds crazy? It's not! It gives the milk a new flavor and most kids love it!

Think you're spending too much time in the kitchen? June 2023. *Guinness World Records* reports Hilda Effiong Bassey (Hilda Baci), a 26-year-old Nigerian chef, holds the record for the longest cooking marathon. She spent 93 hours and 11 minutes cooking over 100 pots of various food during her 4-day cooking marathon.

She wanted to set the record at 100 hours but had 7 minutes deducted for taking extra minutes during one of her early breaks early on in the attempt.

Indian chef Lata Tondon held the previous record when she cooked for 87 hours and 45 minutes in 2019.

The previous record of 87 hours 45 minutes was set by Lata Tondon (India) in 2019.

What it really is. "Barbecue: It's not just a meal, it's a ritual."

     - **Ed Mitchell,** American pitmaster and businessman. Mitchell's frequent media appearances and advocacy for the use of heritage breed pork have earned him the title of the most "famous pitmaster" in North Carolina.

Gordon Ramsay. Some say the British can be too proper and reserved. Not so with Gordon. Here are a few sayings showing his outrageous ingenious creativity using almost everything known in the English language and more,

- "My gran could do better! And she's dead!"

- "This lamb is so undercooked, it's following Mary to school!"

- "This pizza is so disgusting, if you take it to Italy, you'll get arrested."

- "There's enough garlic in here to kill every vampire in Europe."

- "Why did the chicken cross the road? Because you didn't f—ing cook it!"

- "I wouldn't trust you running a bath let alone a restaurant."

- "This fish is so raw, he's still finding Nemo."

- "Chefs are Nutters. They're all self-obsessed, delicate, dainty, insecure little souls, and absolute psychopaths. Every last one of them."

- "You used so much oil, the U.S. wants to invade the f—ing plate."

- "Loo doors without a decent, large hook are as infuriating as a lock that doesn't offer you full protection."

- "I can spot within the first 15 minutes of a young chef in the kitchen whether they're passionate. Cooking with their eyes, their left-and right-hand side, their posture, holding the knife, excitement and developing the palate."

- "I've never been one for pondering or questioning and thinking. Waste of time. Dust yourself down and get back up."

- "This crab is so undercooked I can still hear it singing 'Under the Sea!'"

- "This soufflé has sunk so badly James Cameron wants to make a film about it."

- "Eating out doesn't have to be a formula. Eating out is about having fun."

- "On the personal front obviously, well you know, this industry fragments a lot of families. If there's one thing I've learned with my children, teaching them how to cook early on in life has brought them closer to my industry. So, if they're gonna follow it as a career, they know how to cook."

- "My wife, a schoolteacher, is very disciplined. If you think I'm tough, trust me, and wait till you see when the children are on the naughty step. It's hilarious. So, we decided that I'm going to work like a donkey and provide amazing support for the family."

A self-made man, he's a husband, father, and married to Tana since 1996. They have five wonderful children. He and his wife have helped many various charities giving their time and money to worthwhile causes.

Gordon Ramsay

Tough to clean the Microwave? Fun with vinegar. An easy way to loosen burnt residue, grease, etc., is using vinegar. Take a microwave-safe bowl or jug and add 500ml of water, followed by 2 tablespoons of white vinegar.

Place the bowl into the microwave. Then microwave on full power for 5 minutes, and it should boil and let off steam.

Then after 5 minutes is up, leave the microwave door closed for around 3 minutes trapping the steam inside.

Then, slowly and carefully remove the bowl (it's boiling hot) with an oven glove or mitt and remove the turntable.

Most of the burnt-on food should be loose and easy to remove with a sponge. Rub more for stubborn burnt-on grime and clean the turntable, wipe it all dry, and you're done.

There are also many commercial products you can buy and an interesting one is called, "Angry Mama!" It looks like an angry mama (eyes narrowed, hands on hips, angry look on face, etc.) and it gets your attention as a good reminder to all to clean the microwave after use and be considerate.

Question. How do you know a frugal Scotsman made chocolate chip cookies?

A. You find M&M shells all over the floor.

Recipes. "I read recipes the same way I read science fiction. I get to the end and say to myself, "Well, that's not going to happen."

— Rita Rudner

AI Chef. There are many recipes created by Artificial Intelligence available online these days. We like old recipes that Grandma kept for years. Nevertheless, we had to try it out on an AI recipe generator we randomly found on Buzzfeed (see the link in References at the back of the book). [10]

We told the AI generator we wanted a recipe for lunch for two and the only food we had on hand were garbanzo beans, kale, prawn, and nuts. After several seconds, the AI recipe generator came up with this recipe.

Delicious Prawn and Kale Medley with Garbanzo Beans and Nuts. Servings: 2

Ingredients:

- 200g prawns, peeled and deveined

- 1 cup garbanzo beans, cooked

- 2 cups kale, chopped

- 1/4 cup nuts (e.g., almonds, walnuts, or pistachios), roughly chopped

- 2 tablespoons olive oil

- 2 cloves garlic, minced

- 1/2 teaspoon paprika

- Salt and pepper to taste

- Optional: lemon wedges for serving

Instructions:

1. In a large skillet, heat 1 tablespoon of olive oil over medium heat. Add the prawns and cook for 2-3 minutes per side, until they turn pink and are cooked through. Set it aside.

2. In the same skillet, add the remaining tablespoon of olive oil. Sauté the minced garlic until fragrant, about 1 minute.

3. Add the chopped kale to the skillet and cook for 3-4 minutes, stirring occasionally, until wilted and slightly tender.

4. Stir in the garbanzo beans and cook for another 2 minutes until heated through.

5. Sprinkle paprika, salt, and pepper over the mixture, and stir well to combine all the flavors.

6. Return the cooked prawns to the skillet and gently toss everything together until evenly distributed.

7. Sprinkle the chopped nuts over the top of the dish and cook for an additional minute, allowing the nuts to lightly toast.

8. Serve the prawn and kale medley warm. Garnish with lemon wedges if desired, which can be squeezed over the dish right before eating to add a refreshing citrusy touch.

Serve this delightful prawn and kale medley with a side of fluffy rice or quinoa for a wholesome meal. The flavors and textures of the dish complement rice or quinoa perfectly, creating a satisfying lunch. If you wish to customize the recipe, consider experimenting with different seasonings such as adding a pinch of chili flakes for a spicy kick or substituting the nuts with seeds for variation. Additionally, you can enhance the dish with a squeeze of fresh lemon juice or even a dash of your favorite hot sauce according to your taste preferences. Enjoy your homemade lunch!

Wow! Perhaps the days of flipping through cookbooks are over and done with.

Low and Slow. "The secret to barbecue is low and slow."

-- Jamie Purviance, well-known grill master.

Homegrown. "It's difficult to think anything but pleasant thoughts while eating a homegrown tomato."

-- Lewis Grizzard

If you're lookin', you're not cookin'. "My wife told me I take too long at the barbeque grill! She suggested I take too much time moistening food while I'm cooking!

"That's ridiculous!" I replied and asked, "Based on what?"

Cooking started millions of years ago. Scientists analyzed burnt bone fragments and plant ashes from the Wonderwerk Cave in South Africa and found evidence supporting the control of fire by early humans over 1 million years ago. [11]

Cooking went on from there as anthropologists think widespread cooking fires began about 250,000 years ago when hearths first appeared.

Cooking Riddle. Determine Pizza volume. If you had a pizza with crust thickness "a" and radius "z", how do you determine the volume of the pizza?

Answer p. 99

Banned. I got banned from the secret cooking society…

For spilling the beans...

Veggies. "Vegetables are a must on a diet. I suggest carrot cake, zucchini bread, and pumpkin pie."

      -- Jim Davis

The truth comes out! A man wakes up after a heavy night of drinking to his wife happily cooking breakfast.

Confused, he approaches his daughter for an explanation of last night when he arrived home.

"You kicked in the door when you couldn't get your key in the lock, fell through the table and broke it, and peed your pants."

"Oh No! So then why the heck is she in such a good mood?"

"When she tried to take your pants off to wash them, you slapped her hand away and said, 'Get your hands off me! I'm married!'"

No mistakes. "Chefs don't make mistakes, they make new dishes."

-- Chef Elizabeth Briggs

Watermelon. "Watermelon - it's a good fruit. You eat, you drink, you wash your face."

-- Enrico Caruso

BBQ briskets slowly. Briskets come from the lower chest part of the cow, and since it's a part that is well exercised it is usually a tough piece of meat compared to other parts.

In the early 1800s large cattle owners knew briskets didn't sell as well and they kept the finer parts for the markets, etc. Hardworking cowboys were only given briskets.

The cowboys soon learned a slow-cooked brisket when cooked for a long time was just as good as the good parts, if not better.

Great BBQ. "A great barbecue is a tribute to the backyard heroes who put in the hours to perfect their craft."

- **Tuffy Stone**, American Chef. The Professor of Barbecue

Know how this feels? A husband and wife came back from a long cross-country road trip over 4 days and shared the driving. And there was lots and lots of driving.

The next morning after they returned the day before in the late evening, the husband was making a breakfast of fried eggs for his wife.

Suddenly, his wife bursts into the kitchen. "Careful," she said, "CAREFUL! Put in some more butter! Oh my gosh! You're cooking too much at once. TOO MUCH!

"Turn them! TURN THOSE EGGS NOW!

"You need more butter. Oh my gosh! WHERE are we going to get MORE BUTTER? They're going to STICK! Careful. CAREFUL! I said be CAREFUL!

"You NEVER listen to me when you're cooking! Never! Turn them! Hurry up! Are you CRAZY? Have you LOST your mind?

"Don't forget to salt them. You know you always forget to salt them. Use the Salt. USE THE SALT! THE SALT!"

The husband stared at her and said, "What in the world is wrong with you?! You think I don't know how to fry a couple of eggs?"

"Oh, I just wanted to show you what it feels like when I'm driving."

What's for dinner? "I love cooking dogs and children."

"Say what?!"

"But I hate using commas."

A Celebration! "Barbecue is a celebration of fire and smoke, and the flavors they bring to the table."

- Chris Lilly

You don't mean that?! "My husband's cooking is so bad."

"How bad is it?"

"My husband's cooking is so bad, we usually pray after our food.

Not alone. "No one who cooks, cooks alone.

Even at his or her most solitary moments, a cook in the kitchen is surrounded by generations of cooks past, the advice and menus of cooks present, the wisdom of cookbook writers."

-- Laurie Colwin

Cooking riddle. The grouchy baker. What did the grouchy baker make?

Answer p. 99

BBQ? Confusing origins. More interesting facts. Barbecue seems to come from the Spanish word *barbacoa*, which has its origin in an indigenous American word.

Etymologists believe this to be derived from *barabicu* found in the language of the people of the Caribbean and the Timucua people of Florida. [12]

The Oxford English Dictionary (OED) traces the word to Hispaniola and translates it as a "framework of sticks set upon posts." [13]

Another origin comes from the French *barbe à queue*, meaning "from beard to tail" symbolizing a whole animal being roasted on a spit. [14]

Cooking with wine. "I'd be more likely to cook, if I didn't have to eat my own cooking."

-- Anon.

Prepare the table and the guests too! My husband's was cooking for our guests. He told me to go in and prepare the table.

So, I walked in and told them all about his cooking.

I forgot my wallet! This is a true story about an expensive burger. During the Covid-19 epidemic Dutch Chef, Robbert Jan De Veen a chef at The Daltons in Voorthuizen, Gelderland, Netherlands wanted to break the world record for the most expensive burger on the planet.

He did that and according to the Guinness Book of World Records, he created the most expensive hamburger (single portion) that sold for €5,000 (£4,295 / $5,967), and the new record was achieved on 28 June 2021.

He closed his restaurant but was still making food to take away. During that, he discovered on Facebook that someone had posted and broken the record for the most expensive burger. The burger was huge. Robbert decided he could do it, but it would be a smaller (more classy) sized burger for a single

25

dinner plate and for one person not having to share it because of its size.

He created his own recipe and named the burger "The Golden Boy" and started from scratch. He wanted the burger to be excellent quality and be worth 5,000 Euros.

He first created the bun that would be lightly toasted but soft on the inside and used Dom Pérignon champagne. He covered the bun in gold leaf. When the customer picked up the bun, the customer would have gold fingers.

Chef Robbert described the burger as tasting sweet, sour, salty, bitter, and umami. Robbert admitted it's easy to take super expensive ingredients and make a burger but the challenge he faced was to make sure it was delicious. He wanted those 5 tastes to stand out and be in perfect harmony.

He admits he was nervous serving it fearing he might drop it in front of a crowd, and he did stumble a bit and almost tripped when he served it but managed to hold the plate level without disturbing anything.

Robbert got a lot of free publicity by breaking the record and featuring his skills and he graciously donated the full €5,000 from the first record-setting "Golden Boy" burger to a local food bank that was known to make 1,000 food packages for the families who needed help. [15]

Why do men like to BBQ?

- "I don't know why men like to barbecue so much. Maybe it's the only thing they can cook. Or maybe they're just closet pyromaniacs." — **Cecelia Ahern**, "P.S. I Love You."

- "Men like to barbecue. Men will cook if danger is involved." -- **Rita Rudner**

- "Men like to barbeque since we still have our basic Caveman instinct. Get meat, Start Fire, Cook Meat. It's primal and we must respect it. When men gather around the fire and cook a feast for the tribe (family, buddies, camping or whatever) it's just our primal instinct being fulfilled." – Anon.

- "Raw meat and open flames. That just screams masculinity." – Anon.

27

- "I can't answer everyone, but the reason I like it is because I like the results. BBQ ribs, brisket, pork butt, loin, all of it, are among my favorite things to eat. It also seems to put smiles on other people's faces when they eat it, so I see it as my way to bring happiness to the world." – Anon.

Brits handle waiting in line (queue) well. What do they call three Barbies waiting in a line?

A. BBQ

Try this on Movie Night – Popcorn Pizza! This is an extraordinary pizza, but it sounds a bit weird. Many think you're joking about mentioning it.

Here is a recipe for a Popcorn Pizza. It's not hard to do.

You'll need,

- 4 cups freshly popped popcorn
- 2 cups Mozzarella cheese
- ¼ cup Butter

Dough ingredients,

- 2 cups Sourdough starter (active)
- 1 cup Bread flour
- 1 tsp Salt

Start with the dough and this takes about an hour.

Mix the sourdough starter, bread flour (adding a bit of flour at a time until it takes shape but is still a little sticky), and salt together.

Keep kneading the dough for 30 seconds, flouring lightly. Add a little water if it's too dry.

Put the dough in a lightly floured bowl and cover it with a towel, then set aside for about an hour. (The pizza oven pan or stone needs to be preheated for about an hour. Preheat the oven to 550°F after finishing the dough).

Pizza ingredients.

- Grated mozzarella cheese.
- Popped popcorn.

Flour your work area surface and roll out the dough, flouring it lightly as needed. Put a floured pizza peel, pizza shovel, a pizza paddle, or a pizza slider, underneath the dough.

Add melted butter, then 1 cup of mozzarella cheese, 4 cups popped popcorn, then 1 more cup of mozzarella, and pat it all down.

Bake pizza in the oven at 550° F. for 8-10 minutes.

Remove pizza from oven with a pizza peel and let cool for 5 minutes. You're done and slice it up!

Kitchen sink. I fell asleep beside the kitchen sink.

I feel completely drained now.

Condiment pun. So, I was cooking today...I heated some oil, and fried up some garlic, onion, and chili peppers. Stirred in some chopped tomatoes, added vinegar and sugar, and left it to simmer. Wow! When it was done, it was relish!

Don't try Fugu at home! The Fugu Puffer Fish is considered one of the most difficult dishes to prepare. The Japanese have eaten fugu for centuries. Fugu bones have been found in several shell middens (called kaizuka} from the Jōmon period that dates back more than 2,300 years. [16]

Mistakes have been made in preparing the Fugu fish which has organs containing neurotoxins 1,000 times more deadly than cyanide. Errors can be deadly. The Japanese Emperor by long-established custom does not eat Fugu.

The Japanese reportedly prepare this fish by first dismembering it using special Japanese knives and fish parts hastily separated into 'edible' or 'deadly'. The highly poisonous organs need to be carefully separated to avoid contaminating the toxins onto the edible meat. Only licensed chefs in Japan are permitted to serve it.

Under Japanese law, chefs need at least three or more years of experience before they become licensed to prepare this fish.

The fish's liver is served as a traditional dish named fugu-kimo and most say it is the tastiest part, but it is also the most poisonous. Fugu has become one of the most celebrated dishes in Japanese and Korean cuisine.

Fugu Puffer Fish

Marijuana in the BBQ. I drop a little cannabis in the BBQ whenever I BBQ.

The steaks have never been higher.

Unusual pairing. Whipped cream and potato chips. Just add a dab of whipped cream right on top of a chip and take a bite. You will taste sweetness and crunchiness similar to a crisp waffle and ice cream melting on the top.

Grandma's cooking.

"Grandma's cooking is so good!"

"How good is it?"

"Grandma's cooking is soooo gooood, it'll make you time travel!"

"Time travel??"

"You'll go back four seconds!"

Pound cake. Pound cake got its name because the original recipe called for a pound of each of its four ingredients, sugar, eggs, flour, and butter.

Pound cake was believed first made in Northern Europe in the early 1700s, but the famous recipe was first found in early American cookbooks.

Groaner. Learning about animal-based oils. Did you hear about the chef who never understood how animal-based oils help the cooking process? This chef believes the Lard works in mysterious ways!

Food to avoid. "Avoid nuts. You are what you eat."

-- Jim Davis

Complicated cookbook. One young bachelor said to another bachelor, "I got a cookbook once, but I couldn't do anything with it?"

"Was it too complicated?"

"No, no, I could figure out how to do it but every one of the recipes began the same way – 'Take a clean dish and...'"

Starting out. "I was 32 when I started cooking. Up until then, I just ate."

-- Julia Child

Quick thinking. A slightly overweight woman joined a Diet Club, and she was lamenting that she had gained weight after joining the club.

She said she had made her family's favorite luscious cake during the weekend, and added that they'd eaten half of it at dinner that evening.

Then the next day, she kept staring at the other half, until finally, she cut a thin slice for herself.

As you might guess, one slice led to another, and soon the whole cake had vanished.

She was, of course, very upset about her lack of willpower, and how she knew her husband would be so disappointed.

We all felt for her, until someone asked what her husband said when he found out.

She smiled broadly and quipped, "He never found out. I made another cake and ate half of that too."

A few observations about food.

- "If someone else is paying for it, food just tastes a lot better." **- Gilbert Gottfried**

- "Anything is good if it's made of chocolate." **- Jo Brand**

- "Fettuccini alfredo is macaroni and cheese for adults." **- Mitch Hedberg**

- "I could talk about food all day. I love good food." **- Tom Brady**

- "Initially let your food do the talking. You'll be surprised how far you go in a short period of time." **- Gordon Ramsay**

- "A human being is primarily a bag for putting food into." - **George Orwell**

- "Popcorn for breakfast! Why not? It's a grain. It's like, like, grits, but with high self-esteem." - **James Patterson**

- "Seize the moment. Remember all those women on the Titanic who waved off the dessert cart." - **Erma Bombeck**

- "The only think I like better than talking about food is eating." - **John Walters**

Have you ever wondered why crackers have little holes? During baking, little holes must be made before baking since they are needed to stop internal air bubbles from ruining the product.

Husband kitchen mishaps.

- My husband used a square chopping board to cover a wok thinking the wok needed a lid. Of course, it didn't fit so he used cellophane to cover the whole thing.

- My husband boiled potatoes in a cake tin.

- My husband asked me how long it takes to cook two-minute noodles.

- My husband cooked dinner and while he was cooking, he decided to water my plants in the kitchen. I thought that was very considerate. But he watered the fake plants too.

        -- Anon.

Cooking relieves stress. The National Library of Medicine reports that scientific studies show that baking and cooking help relieve stress. [17] It's often suggested as an activity to help with anxiety and depression.

Experts say the soothing act of cooking helps boost confidence and keeps thoughts focused to ultimately avoid negative self-talk. [18]

Dolly's weakness. "My weaknesses have always been food and men - in that order."

  -- Dolly Parton

Captions for Instagram pictures.

- "Grillin' and chillin' at the BBQ party!"

- "BBQ isn't just about the food; it's about the love and passion that goes into every bite."
-

- "Sauce boss, ruling the grill with a smokin' attitude."

- "Bringing the heat and meat to the backyard BBQ fiesta!"

- "Grill masters don't just cook food; they weave stories and create culinary masterpieces."

- "In the world of BBQ, patience is rewarded with tender, melt-in-your-mouth goodness.

- "Get ready for a grill-a-coaster of flavors!"

- "It's not just grillin', it's a way of life."

- "Grill it, thrill it, and enjoy every tasty bit!"

- "BBQ is a celebration of simplicity, where quality ingredients shine."

- "Each bite of perfectly grilled meat tells a story of dedication and skill."

- "Sizzle, smoke, and savor the BBQ goodness."

- "BBQ vibes and good times, that's what we're all about."

- "BBQ is a delicious journey that starts with a flicker of flame and ends with a plate full of happiness."

- "BBQ is more than just a meal; it's a timeless tradition that connects us to our roots."

- "Grilling like a boss and bringing the sauce!"

- "When life hands you BBQ sauce, slather it on everything!"

- "Let's get this BBQ party started and make some grillicious memories!"

- "Time to turn up the heat and spice up the BBQ game."

- "Grilling brings people together, creating unforgettable moments and lifelong memories."

- "BBQ is an invitation to slow down, savor the moment, and appreciate the simple pleasures of life."

- "The grill is my happy place, where I can unleash my culinary creativity and let flavors come alive."

- "BBQ is an expression of love, shared among friends and family."

A $12,000 PIZZA! The most expensive pizza in the world is named "Louis XIII" and was made in Salerno, Italy, was priced at $12,000, and was made by Chef Renato Viola. He did it for a small number of customers.

The diameter was 20cm (roughly 8") and was made for 2 people so if you split it, it's only $6,000 per person.

He makes the dough from organic Arabian flour dusting it with Murray River pink salt and he allows the pizza dough to rest at various stages and overall, it takes him 72 hours to finish the dough before it is ready for cooking.

So, what's on it? The toppings are three highly expensive and rare types of caviar known as Oscietra Royal Prestige, Kaspia Oscietra Royal Classic from the Iranian coast, and Kaspia Beluga.

He also has Norwegian lobster and 7 types of cheese on this highly expensive pizza.

Chef Renato serves the pizza with special beverages such as Champagne Krug Clos du Mesnil 1995 to complement the lobster and caviar. There's also a brandy -- Carta Real Sanches Romate Finos brandy. And, you guessed it, Louis XIII cognac which many consider the finest cognac in existence.

Upon your request, the pizza can be cooked and served at your home.

Perhaps someday, the major pizza chains will catch on to this idea but seems pizza delivery may be made by fully guarded armored cars!

Another world record has been set for commercial pizzas. If you want to order a special pizza commercially, the world's most expensive commercially available pizza recognized by

Guinness World Records costs US$2,700. [19] At the time of this writing, we are not sure it's still available.

The record was set by Industry Kitchen in New York, New York, (in the big apple of course) on April 24, 2017. It has black squid ink dough and is topped with white Stilton cheese from the UK, French foie gras and truffles, Ossetra caviar from the Caspian Sea, Almas caviar, and 24K gold leaves. [20] You want onion rings with that?

Tired of cooking in the kitchen? "Teach a man to Barbecue and you'll feed him for the summer."

-- Anon.

Great dinner Mom! A family just got back from their vacation and didn't have a lot in the house for dinner. Scrambling through what was available, a very innovative and creative mom served a dinner of frozen pizza, yogurt tubes, and canned peaches.

Their 4-year-old looked at his plate and said "Mom, you're the best cook ever!"

Cooking Riddle. Outer space cooking. What did the astronaut cook in his skillet?

Answer p. 99

Keep that BBQ brush handy! One night in Fayette County, Pennsylvania, a couple was asleep in their mobile home when the woman was awakened by a loud knocking at the door, It was her ex-boyfriend who showed up wanting his $6 Walmart card back claiming there was still some money on it.

Arguing woke up the man and a confrontation occurred, The ex-boyfriend looked like he was walking away, but he was actually going to his car. He immediately returned with a full-length Japanese katana sword in a bamboo case. [21]

This made the mobile homeowner do some quick thinking, "I'm thinking, what am I going to do?" he said. "The only thing I grabbed is a spatula."

He grabbed a wire BBQ brush he used to clean his grill with as it was the only weapon of defense he could come up with at that instant.

En-garde! A duel ensued. The man had cuts from the sword that were stitched up with 12 stitches. He told the police he had to defend himself with that wire BBQ brush (it was all he could grab!) and he hit the ex-boyfriend with one good strike across the head and that was all it took. The old boyfriend ran away after being hit with it! [22]

The old boyfriend was later arrested and charged with aggravated assault and other charges. [23]

Condiments. "I'm a great cook if you cover my cooking in condiments to the point where you can only taste the condiments."

-- Anon.

Air Fryer. "Let's buy an air fryer. What could be less in calories than fried air."

-- Anon.

Ups and Downs of Air Frying. Air fryers are efficient and highly popular in homes, but they haven't been as popular in restaurants.

Air fryers are highly popular since you can get the crispiness of frying with a lot less oil and therefore less calories.

They tend to be faster and more convenient for small portions and reheating.

Many say a combination of having both an air fryer and conventional stove and oven seems to work best.

Many doctors say air-fried foods are better for you since air frying is healthier than frying foods in oil. It cuts calories by 70% to 80% and has a lot less fat. [24]

It's been found that air frying may cut down on the harmful effects of frying some foods in oil. That's because there is a reaction that happens when frying potatoes in oil or other starch foods that produces the chemical acrylamide, which has been linked to getting cancer. One research study shows that air frying lowers the amount of acrylamide in fried potatoes by 90%. [25]

Although many people say the air fryer delivers a great fried food taste that many of us love, some reports say restaurant chefs don't like the reduced taste quality they sometimes get with it compared to the old fashion oven method.

Air fryers, in general, have a smaller capacity (although larger ones are available for commercial restaurants), some chefs say there are more commercial uses with a large conventional oven.

On the lighter side,

What do you call an air fryer that can't fry?

A. An air liar.

*

How do you know if someone loves their air fryer?

Don't worry, they'll tell you.

*

What is the best thing to make in an air fryer?

Air-vrything.

*

What do you call a couple of potatoes who meet in an air fryer?

Friend fries.

*

I tried to make a joke about air fryers, but it just didn't fry.

*

I'm really loving my air fryer. It's fry-day every day.

*

I can't stop raving about my air fryer. It's definitely an air-replaceable kitchen appliance.

*

I've been trying to eat healthier, so I traded in my deep fryer for an air fryer. I'm just fryin' to be healthier.

*

What do you call an overly confident air fryer?

Full of hot air.

*

I'm making air-fried chicken tonight. I don't have a recipe, so I guess I'll have to wing it.

Greasy situation – true story. One of the older and experienced chefs in a fast-paced restaurant slipped and his elbow and parts of his forearm were unfortunately burned in a deep fryer -- but not too badly. The sous chef rushed over and immediately gave him medical attention.

Nearby, a new young cook who most of the people working in the kitchen didn't really know awkwardly tried to make the tension ease and said, *"Now that's what I call elbow grease!"*

Everyone in the kitchen stopped in their tracks, then as if on cue, everyone burst out laughing and the new cook later became one of the favorites on the staff.

An art form. "Barbecue is the only art form that can be eaten."

-- Anon.

Fat-free frying. Outside a restaurant, there was a sign advertising "Fat-free free French fries".

"Hey, that sounds great!" said the health-conscious man, and ordered some.

To his disappointment, he saw the cook pull a basket of fries from the deep fryer. The potatoes were dripping with oil as the cook put them in the box.

The man said, "Wait a minute, those don't look fat free!"

"They sure are," the cook said. "We only charge for the potatoes, the fat is free."

Like a woman. "Barbecue sauce is like a beautiful woman. If it's too sweet, it's bound to be hiding something."

> **- Lyle Lovett**

The very first one. "He was a bold man that first ate an oyster."

> **-- Jonathan Swift**

A few facts about flavor enhancers. Most everyone is familiar with MSG (monosodium glutamate). At one time, it was thought to be bad for you but that has been debunked by the FDA. [26]

MSG was discovered for food use by chemist Kikunae Ikeda when he found that kelp from the sea held a salty flavor because of the chemical known as L-glutamate.

He found that when he combined L-glutamate with sodium, it actually triples the salty taste. A good result from that is it tends to make people use less sodium.

Another flavor enhancer, **honey** takes on flavors from specific flower nectar. There are those with amazing taste buds who sometimes can detect certain bouquet scents in the honey and consequently honey actually has various tastes like fine wines.

For example, manuka honey is from the manuka tree which is indigenous to New Zealand and some parts of coastal Australia, but is today produced globally. It has a strong, earthy aroma and flavor and is commonly used as a sugar substitute. [27]

That's because honey is two times sweeter than sugar and is used to reduce sugar content in recipes while adding distinctive flavors as well as enhancing the flavors of other ingredients. Some add honey to salad dressings to increase the viscosity.

Citric acid is used as a flavor enhancer adding tartness, refreshing tastes, and acidic tastes, all adding flavor to foods and drinks. Chefs use it to offset overly sweet ingredients.

Corn Syrup (high in fructose) adds sweetness to marshmallows, pecan pies, peanut brittle, and also gives them more texture.

Salt, also known as sodium chloride, chemically stimulates your tastebuds much more than other salts, such as potassium chloride. In small amounts, salt stimulates other tastes and flavors, such as the sweet taste, by suppressing bitter tastes and that's why a bit of salt is added to cookie or cake recipes.

Rodney may be exaggerating a bit.

"My wife is the worst cook in the world. She gave our son alphabet soup, and he spelled out HELP!"

"My wife can't cook at all. If I leave dental floss in the kitchen, the roaches hang themselves, and the flies chip in to fix the screen door!"

-- Rodney Dangerfield

An old one about Bubba cooking a steak. Each Friday night after work, Bubba would fire up his outdoor grill and cook a venison steak. But all of Bubba's neighbors were Catholic....and since it was Lent, they were forbidden from eating meat on Friday.

The delicious aroma from the grilled venison steaks was causing such a problem for the Catholic faithful that they finally talked to their priest.

The Priest came to visit Bubba and suggested that he become a Catholic. After several classes and much study, Bubba attended Mass and as the priest sprinkled holy water over him, the priest chanted, 'You were born a Baptist, and raised a Baptist, but now you are a Catholic.'

Bubba's neighbors were greatly relieved, until Friday night arrived, and the wonderful aroma of grilled venison again filled the neighborhood.

The Priest was called immediately by the neighbors and as he rushed into Bubba's yard clutching a rosary preparing to scold him, he stopped and watched in amazement.

Bubba stood there clutching a small bottle of holy water which he carefully sprinkled over the grilling meat and chanted, "You were born a deer, you were raised a deer, but now you are a catfish."

Two choices. "As a child, my family's menu consisted of two choices: take it or leave it.

-- Buddy Hackett

Only an Australian Santa.

"What would you like for Christmas little girl?"

Little girl: "A Barbie!"

On Christmas morning the little girl woke up and found a small BBQ grill under the tree.

The broken glass. Joe was groggy and hungover in the morning after a long evening out with his friends and knocked over a glass in the kitchen. He called out, "Darn! Honey, I broke a glass in the kitchen."

"It's okay, dear, I'll be there with a broom."

"Don't rush, it's not an emergency. You can come on foot."

Joe should be feeling better in a week or so.

Kitchen riddle. I get hot but I never sweat.

I cook things but I'm not a chef.

I have a door, but you don't go through me.

I can sometimes clean myself but I'm not a person.

I can be gas or electric but I'm not a car.

Answer p. 100

The Scotsman and his wife. A Scotsman and his wife walked past a swanky new restaurant.

"Did you smell that food?" she asked. "Wonderful!"

Being the 'kind-hearted Scotsman', he thought, "What the hell, I'll treat her."

So, they walked past it again.

Leftovers? A husband was watching a cooking show. The host said you can use leftover beer to make battered chicken wings... The husband paused with a wondering look on his face.

"What's wrong, dear?" his wife asked.

"What the hell?! I haven't ever heard of leftover beer.

Senses. John was a simple tailor who had a small shop that didn't have much business and usually struggled to make ends meet. His shop was right next door to an exclusive French restaurant.

One day in the mail John got a bill from the restaurant for a hundred dollars for "enjoyment of food." He went next door to inquire about this strange bill.

He told the chef next door that he hadn't ever eaten at the restaurant and the bill was ridiculous.

Pierre, the restaurant owner told him, "You are enjoying the aroma of our fabulous food so you should pay us for it."

John shook his head, threw the bill on the floor, and walked out.

Pierre sued John for the unpaid bill and told the judge, "Every day during lunch time this tailor sits outside his shop smelling our beautiful food while he eats very poor food. We are adding to the enhancement of his plain food, and we should be compensated."

The judge then asked John what he had to say. John stood up, put his hand in his pocket, and jingled the few coins inside.

After a bit, the Judge asked, "What are you doing?"

John replied, "Well it's simple really, I'm paying for the smell of his food with the sound of my money."

That's a lot of beef? Many years ago, when McDonald's first opened, they used to post on their golden arches how many burgers the chain sold and occasionally you would notice the signs were changed from "Over 5 million sold" to Over 6 million sold, etc.

As of the time of this book, McDonalds sells roughly 6.48 million burgers per day, and over 2 billion per year!

By the way, they also sell 9 million pounds of fries per day.

Let them fight it out. "Part of the secret of a success in life is to eat what you like and let the food fight it out inside."

    -- Mark Twain

Kitchen odors. "The best way to avoid kitchen odors is to eat out."

    -- Phyllis Diller

Original "Sh*t on a Shingle" There are many names for this well-known dish from "Sh*t on a Shingle", "Same ol' Stuff", "Save our Stomachs", etc.

An early record of S.O.S was in the Manual of Army Cooks in 1910 and perhaps is the first published recipe for S.O.S. It was simply chipped beef (a dried meat product designed for the battlefield) and called for evaporated milk (since that could be carried easily and didn't sour), lard, and beef stock. It was basically, making a sauce, adding meat, and serving over bread.

The Navy had its own SOS that was slightly varied since tomatoes were added with other fresh vegetables, fresh ground beef, and nutmeg.

Do you want to surprise everyone by serving the original SOS for dinner? Here's a recipe very similar to the original 1910 Army Manual recipe.

S.O.S. recipe for two people.

- 4 oz butter

- 4 tbsp flour

- 1 cup milk

- 1 cup beef stock

- 3 oz. package of chipped beef, cut into about 1-inch ribbons.

- 2 slices of white bread

- Black pepper.

Sear the beef until the edges start to curl over medium-high heat for about 2 minutes then remove it and put it aside. Toast 2 slices of bread.

Using the same pan that you seared the beef, melt the butter. Once melted, whisk in the flour a bit at a time to make your roux. It should start to bubble in 4 minutes or so. Once it bubbles, stir in the milk and beef stock and let it thicken in about 5-9 minutes.

Then add the beef you had put aside and put in black pepper to your taste. Put the toast on a plate and pour the creamed chipped beef evenly over the shingle.

Add vegetables as you wish and that's it! Real, authentic SOS!

S.O.S.

Shortcut to good health. If politicians really want to make radical changes to America's health long-term, all they have to do is triple the price of sugar and salt."

-- Jamie Oliver

Strength. "Strength is the determination and ability to break a chocolate bar into four pieces with your bare hands - and then eat just one of the pieces."

-- Judith Viorst

Groaner. I started cooking spaghetti. Just to pasta time.

Rocky cake riddle. What would a cake baked by a geologist be called?

Answer p. 100

Barbeque sauce. "Barbecue sauce is like a beautiful woman. If it's too sweet, it's bound to be hiding something."

   -- Lyle Lovett, Grammy Award-winning country singer.

It's about others. "If you are a chef, no matter how good a chef you are, it's not good cooking for yourself; the joy is in cooking for others - it's the same with music."

   -- will.i.am

Say again? A man had Facebook friends all across the Caribbean. He had one friend in Cuba and many all across Jamaica.

One day the Cuban friend is traveling abroad near the man's home and asks if he can stop by for dinner while he's there. The man thinks this is a fantastic idea and starts cooking when his wife walks in.

"Hey, what's up?" his wife asks.

"One of my Facebook friends is in the area and we're having him over for dinner."

"Sounds great. Whatcha makin'?"

"No, it's the guy from Cuba."

Would you care for a few nuts and bee vomit? Honeybees produce honey by gathering and then refining the sugary secretions of plants (primarily floral nectar) or the secretions of other insects, like the honeydew of aphids. [28]

This refinement takes place both within individual bees, through regurgitation and enzymatic activity. When it is stored in the hive, water evaporates to give it a concentration of the honey's sugars until it is thick and viscous. [29]

Lightly drizzle amber honey on your nuts of choice, and eat that or bake in the oven and enjoy a sweet and salty snack the whole family will enjoy.

Two nuts. Q. What did the almond say to the walnut?

"I like you since we're both nuts!"

What everyone needs. "All you need is love. But a little chocolate now and then doesn't hurt."

-- Charles M. Schulz

Damn fish! The preacher's wife goes to the store to get something to cook for dinner. She walks up to the seafood counter and asks, "What's the special today?"

"Dam fish", says the clerk.

"Excuse me, sir, but you know I'm the preacher's wife and you shouldn't use those words."

Embarrassed, the clerk says, "No, no, no. They were caught by the river dam, so they're called 'dam fish.'"

The preacher's wife takes 3 fish, finishes her shopping, heads home, and starts preparing dinner.

The preacher arrives home, smells dinner cooking and goes into the kitchen. "What smells so good?", the preacher asks his wife.

"Dam fish!" she exclaims.

"Excuse me honey, but you know I'm a preacher and you shouldn't use that language."

"No dear. They were caught by the river dam, so they're called dam fish." she informs him.

"Well, I'm very sorry dear but the Bishop contacted me and he's coming over for dinner tonight. Do you have enough?"

"You and your no-notice invites, but I understand, he's the bishop so luckily I have more since I bought 3 fish."

The bishop arrives and they sit down at the table. After saying grace, the preacher says "Honey. Please pass the dam fish."

The bishop smiles and says, "Hey! I'm so tired of being with boring people who are overly polite. Pass the f*cking potatoes!"

Leftovers. "The most remarkable thing about my mother is that for thirty years she served the family nothing but leftovers. The original meal has never been found."

— Calvin Trillin

A special place. "Everybody likes to have a place to think, to meditate, to eat a burrito."

-- Sherman Alexie

Normal BBQ routine.

- The wife buys the food.

- The wife makes small party food, appetizers, and a large salad, and prepares all of the vegetables, as well as dessert.

- The wife prepares the meat for cooking, places it on a tray along with the necessary cooking utensils and sauces, and takes it to the man who is lounging beside the grill - beer in hand telling barbecue jokes.

- Then there is a dramatic and important moment in time – the husband places the meat on the grill.

- The wife goes inside to organize the plates and cutlery and while doing that she smells something burning! There's fire and huge amounts of smoke coming out of the grill! She trots out and tells the husband the meat is burning.

- The husband thanks her and asks her to bring him another beer.

- The husband takes the meat off the grill and hands it to the wife.

- The wife continues preparing the table with plates, utensils, sauces, appetizers, bread, condiments, and more and sets it all out on the table.

- The wife clears the table at the end of the dinner, and does the dishes while everyone compliments the husband on everything and his great cooking, giving much praise and thanks.

- They continue to drink telling lots of jokes and laughing while the wife continues her cleanup.

- The guests leave and the husband asks the wife how she enjoyed "her night off" and she gives him an annoyed look.

- The husband concludes there's just no pleasing a woman!

How you can tell? "You can tell a lot about a fellow's character by his way of eating jellybeans."

-- Ronald Reagan

The famous Franklin Barbecue in Austin Texas. It's owned by Aaron and Stacy Franklin who opened a small barbecue trailer on the side of an interstate road in Austin in 2009. Today customers wait for hours in long lines to get their food.

Celebrities like Jimmy Kimmel, Anthony Bourdain, and even President Obama have been there and tried their delicious food. Obama has the indistinct honor to be the very first one ever to cut in line to get his order in July 2014. [30]

According to reports, Obama ended up paying around $300 for his own order, and an additional amount more (that was not disclosed) to cover the people he cut in line. [31]

Aaron has been inducted into the American Royal Barbecue Hall of Fame in 2020.

Q. Why did the chef quit?

A. They cut his celery.

German Chocolate Cake. How does the recipe for German chocolate cake begin?

A. First, invade ze kitchen.

Unusual sweet and salty combos. Apple slices and peanut butter taste great to most people. An unusual twist is to try apple slices salted with a small dash of pepper for spice.

Another unusual salty-sweet combination is soy sauce on vanilla ice cream. Sounds bad at first but surprisingly, it's not that bad!

Consider wrapping prosciutto around melon slices or just eating them side by side for a nice salty-sweet taste.

This next one sounds absolutely crazy but if you are ever stuck for coming up with an unusual sandwich that you want people to talk about, try a peanut butter and sliced dill pickle sandwich.

Hungry pickle lovers will be impressed. At first you might think the sandwich is going to be a soggy mess. But the vinegar from the pickle does not ruin the sandwich. The sandwich holds together because of the smoothness and viscosity of the peanut butter. It has a highly unusual taste that's sweet and salty and totally different. It's amazing for those who like dill pickles.

Finally, most know that McDonald's serves honey sauce with chicken nuggets. Most like fries with nuggets. Here's a twist. Try offering honey as a dip for French fries to add sweetness to French fries.

Teach fishing. "Cook a man a fish and you feed him for a day. But teach a man to fish and you get rid of him for the whole weekend." – Anon.

Egg boil riddle. You want to boil a two-minute egg. If you only have a three-minute timer (hourglass), a four-minute timer and a five-minute timer can you boil the egg for only two minutes?

Answer p. 100

Cooking for life. "If a child plays sport early in childhood, and doesn't give it up, he will play sport for the rest of his life. And if children have a connection with, and are involved in the preparation of the food they eat, then it will be normal for them to cook these kind of meals, and they will go on cooking them for the rest of their lives."

-- **Ferran Adria**, Renowned Spanish Chef

Whasamaddayou? Did you hear about the Italian chef that died?

He pasta way. We cannoli do so much.

His legacy will become a pizza history.

Groaner. Why did the pastry chef get arrested?

For baking and entering.

Start of the Southern BBQ. In the Pre-Civil War period, Southerners preferred to eat pork over beef by a 5 to one margin.

You may wonder why such a big margin? It was because pigs were easier to raise than cattle, and Barbecuing pork was highly popular at that time in the deep South, and it continues to the present day.

For what it's worth – a few unusual food facts.

- Pistachios aren't nuts—they are actually fruits. They are known as "drupes" which come from trees and the pistachio is the fruit of the tree inside a hard shell.

- The very first food eaten in outer space was applesauce. John Glenn ate applesauce on the Friendship 7 flight in 1962.

- A rose is a rose…well, maybe not. Many fruits are in the rose family technically called the Rosacea family. The Rosacea family include raspberries and strawberries. There are fruit trees also in the Rosacea family such as the apple tree and also these trees: pear, plum, cherry, apricot, and peach.

- Frank Epperson in the early 1900s invented the popsicle when he was just 11 years old. It happened on a winter night in 1905, Frank mixed a soft drink made with soda water powder and water and left it outside overnight and it froze. He called it the "Ep-sicle" and was granted a US Patent on his invention in 1924 and later sold it. He also invented "High-Dry" which was a powered drink mix that eventually was developed by others who turned it into Kool-Aid and Tang.

- Bad eggs float. Rotten eggs float. If you ever wonder if an egg is bad, see if it floats in a glass of water. If it floats, don't eat it.

- Cucumbers are 95% water, watermelons are 92% water, and surprisingly potatoes are 80% water.

- Tonic water glows in the dark under ultraviolet light. Turn out the lights and shine an ultraviolet light (a black light) and it will glow with a bright blue color. This is it contains quinine which absorbs the ultraviolet light from the black light and then emits a wonderful blue light.

Bad cooking. Husband: "My cooking is so bad."

Dinner guest: "How bad is it?"

Husband: "My cooking is so bad, my last guest thought my Thanksgiving dinner was to commemorate the Great Chicago Fire."

What celebrities have said about food.

- "My doctor told me I had to stop throwing intimate dinners for four unless there are three other people." - **Orson Welles**

- "Unless you are a pizza, the answer is yes, I can live without you." - **Bill Murray**

- "There's nothing better than cake but more cake." - **Harry S. Truman**

- "He who does not mind his belly, will hardly mind anything else." - Samuel Johnson

- "The only time to eat diet food is while you're waiting for the steak to cook." - **Julia Child**

- "Never eat more than you can lift." - **Miss Piggy**

- "Always serve too much hot fudge sauce on hot fudge sundaes. It makes people overjoyed and puts them in your debt." - **Judith Olney**

- "Only the pure in heart can make a good soup." – **Ludwig van Beethoven**

- "Health food may be good for the conscience, but Oreos taste a hell of a lot better." - Robert Redford

- "The best comfort food will always be greens, cornbread, and fried chicken." - **Maya Angelou**

- "As long as there's pasta and Chinese food in the world, I'm okay." - **Michael Chang**

- "I only drink Champagne on two occasions, when I am in love and when I am not." - **Coco Chanel**

- "Spaghetti can be eaten most successfully if you inhale it like a vacuum cleaner." - **Sophia Loren**

- "Absolutely eat dessert first. The thing that you want to do the most, do that." - **Joss Whedon**

- "I eat steak primarily. That's pretty much what my diet consists of. Sometimes I supplement that with other steaks." – **Navy Seal Jocko Willink**

- "Food is celebratory. People who don't cook don't know how much fun they're missing." - **Leo Buscaglia**

- "I can eat two large pizzas and a tray of brownies in one sitting. I'm not sharing that. We can get another one, but I ain't sharing." - **Dwayne Johnson**

- "Older people shouldn't eat health food, they need all the preservatives they can get." - **Robert Orben**

How to cook Tigerfish. If you want to ever surprise the heck out of your dinner guests. You can have an African Tigerfish shipped to you (there are several sites online that ship Goliath Tigerfish to the US and other countries).

You may wonder, what is a tigerfish? Tigerfish are the African version of the South American Piranha. They are found in the Congo River system and Lake Tanganyika. The largest one on record weighed 70 kg (154 pounds). [32]

Tigerfish are exceptionally ferocious and have been known to eat crocodiles and sometimes (although rarely) people.

Tigerfish are whitefish, and their meat is tender and tasty. They are often grilled, fried, baked, and prepared in a similar manner to tilapia.

There are not many finer fish dishes than the pickled white meat of the tigerfish.

Here is just one recipe from Africa for pickled tigerfish. The preparation time is about 30 minute and about an hour to cook. You can eat it hot or cold.

Ingredients

- ½ cup vegetable oil for frying

- 3 pounds Kariba Tiger Fish OR alternatively; Cod fillets, Hake or Yellow Tail cut into 2-to-3-ounce portions

- salt to taste

- 2 large onions, peeled and sliced into rings.

- 2 cloves garlic, chopped.

- 8 whole black peppercorns

- 4 whole Allspice berries

- 3 or 4 Bay leaves

- 1 red Chile pepper seeded and sliced lengthwise.

- 2 cups Red wine vinegar

- ½ cup water

- ½ cup packed brown sugar, or to taste

- 2 tablespoons Curry powder or use Curry Leaves.

- 1 teaspoon ground Turmeric

- 2 teaspoons ground Cumin

- 2 teaspoons ground Coriander.

Heat the oil in a large skillet over medium-high heat. Season the fish with salt and put it in the skillet. Fry on both sides until fish is browned and cooked through, and depending on the size of the fish it takes about 5 minutes per side.

Remove from the skillet and set aside.

Fry the onions and garlic in the same skillet over medium heat until translucent. Add peppercorns, allspice berries, bay leaves, and red chili pepper. Pour in the vinegar and water and bring it all to a boil. Stir in the brown sugar until dissolved. Season with curry powder, turmeric, cumin and coriander. Taste and adjust the sweetness as desired.

Layer pieces of fish and the pickling mixture in a serving dish. Pour the liquid over so the top layer is covered.

Allow to cool then cover and refrigerate for at least 24 hours before serving.

Another popular method to cook tigerfish is to finely mince the meat to create exceptionally tasty fish cakes.

Tigerfish

Sauna steamed food. Have you heard about a Sauna that serves food?

Their specialty is steamed mussels.

Round ice cubes last longer than square ice cubes. You may know that many upscale commercial bars use round ice cubes. Why? It's because round-shaped ice melts slower since it exposes less surface area for the same amount of volume as an ice cube.

If you wonder about that, take two ice cubes about the same size and round off the corners of one of them. Put them in a glass and see what cube lasts longer.

You can search online to get round ice ball molds almost anywhere.

Hawaiian Pizza. Burnt my Hawaiian pizza today…

Should have cooked it on Aloha temperature.

Alligator. What's the best way to cook an alligator?

In a crock pot.

A pancake story. A young teenage boy who hadn't cooked very much decided to make pancakes one morning all by himself. He didn't realize that it's normal to use a non-stick pan (believe it not).

When it came time to flip the pancakes, they were stuck of course, but he kept at it trying to scrape it off before it burned too badly. He wound up flinging burnt pancakes all over the kitchen!

Wise words. An old chef told his grandson, "There is a battle between two wolves inside us all. You will hear them more as you grow.

"One wolf is bad. It is anger, jealousy, greed, resentment, inferiority, lies, and ego. The other is good. It is joy, peace, love, hope, humility, kindness, empathy, and truth."

The grandson pondered that then asked, "Grandfather, which wolf wins?"

The old chef quietly replied, "The one you feed."

-- Anon.

Woman in a restaurant. "OMG! There's a hair in my food!

"I'm gonna vomit!

"Ack, ack.

"I'm never coming here ag...oh wait!

"It's mine.

"Never mind..."

Wine pairing. "My favorite wine pairing is me with a bottle of wine."

-- Anon.

Forced to eat. "Once, during Prohibition, I was forced to live for days on nothing but food and water."

-- W. C. Fields

Downsides of cooking.

1. Hoping the stove doesn't burst into flames.
2. Wondering how much salt is enough.
3. Thinking of all the dishes you have to get washed.

Loving food. "Never trust a skinny cook."

-- **Iain Hewitson,** Australian celebrity chef.

Transformer Decepticons. In the middle of the night a wife found her husband searching the kitchen and holding a gun.

"What the heck are you doing?" She was shocked!

"Quiet woman! I'm hunting Decepticons!" the husband whispered.

She put her hands on her hips. "You've been sleepwalking again! There are no such thing as Decepticons!"

The husband woke up, blinked, and realized how stupid he looked. "I guess you're right! Wow! I must look like an idiot!"

She laughed.

The husband laughed.

The toaster laughed.

The husband shot the toaster.

Choosing plates and palates. Did you know that generally, round, white plates bring out sweeter flavors. [33]

Also, a black angular or cornered plate brings out spicy and salty flavors. And, as crazy as this sounds, studies have been done and discovered that red plates generally reduce the amount you eat. [34]

The art of cooking. Cooking is like painting or writing a song. Just as there are only so many notes or colors, there are only so many flavors - it's how you combine them that sets you apart.

-- Wolfgang Puck

Differences: Homemade pizza v. Restaurant pizza. Ever wonder why restaurant pizza tastes better than homemade?

Most say it's because restaurant pizza has ovens that can reach 900°F, or even hotter. The results are perfectly crisp and chewy crusts with a few charred spots.

Another reason, "Pizza toppings are also packed with a compound called glutamate, which can be found in the tomatoes, cheese, pepperoni and sausage. When glutamate hits our tongues, it tells our brains to get excited – and to crave more of it. [35]

There are many other reasons. Restaurants use a thin layer of tomato sauce. Homemade pizza may use too much sauce that adds weight to a pizza, and the result is the dough won't rise as well under the weight of the sauce that results in a soggy crust.

Most restaurants have the sauce thinly masking the dough and not predominate over the rest of the toppings. A thinner layer also heats the dough through better.

Definition of "Hangry" When you are at a restaurant and order way too much food that you really can't eat, then you get angry when it isn't served in 4 minutes.

Unwritten cooking rules.

- There is no such thing as too much garlic or onions when cooking.

- Grilled Cheese and Tomato soup must always be eaten together.

- An elaborately prepared dinner must be enjoyed by candlelight when possible.

- If you dirty it, you clean it…put the dishes in the dishwasher, or wash it after you are done.

- Follow directions first. Experiment later.

- Be prepared for last-minute guests.

- Cook for people and they will know you love them, and they'll remember it long after you're gone.

Diets. "A balanced diet is a cookie in each hand."

   -- Barbara Johnson

Roof BBQ. Why don't people barbecue on their roofs?

The steaks are too high!

I had a taste for kielbasa!   This happened in the UK. A young Polish guy who recently lost his builder job, had a few too many at the local pub. He wound up at his sister's place and was hungry for sausage, so he lit a barbeque in the living room to cook a few sausages. He used a portable disposable BBQ and got it going with lighter fluid. [36]

Running low on wood for the fire, he ripped three internal doors off their hinges and tore up floorboards at the house.

He was sober enough to disable the smoke alarms but left the home after realizing it's not a good idea to tear apart your sister's residence. He didn't get far though and was arrested nearby.

At the court hearing, it was hard for him to not plead guilty since he disabled the fire alarms. He had burned a large hole in the floor and other parts of the residence.

He was jailed for three years for arson. Luckily no one was injured. [37]

Facing the truth. "Let's face it, a nice creamy chocolate cake does a lot for a lot of people; it does for me.

-- **Audrey Hepburn**

"Old Hickory" President, Andrew Jackson (nicknamed "Old Hickory") got that nickname since he was tough as old hickory wood, and known for his hickory-fired barbecues.

Hickory is a good choice if you are having a long BBQ. It burns clean and has a smell a bit sweet and tends to smell like bacon.

Love. "The most indispensable ingredient of all good home cooking: love for those you are cooking for."

-- Sophia Loren

Don't mess with Granny. Granny tells Grandpa that if he walks across the kitchen floor one more time after she mops, she's going to do something drastic.

Grandpa ignores her, and goes into the kitchen to get a beer, then tracks water into the living room and sits back in the recliner with dirty wet slippers in the air.

Granny mops the kitchen floor again.

Grandpa then goes back into the kitchen thinking he forgot something and walked on the kitchen floor again getting the floor dirty. Grandpa forgets what he was going to get and tracks water into the living room and sits back in the recliner putting his dirty wet slippers in the air.

Granny tells Grandpa that if he walks across the kitchen floor one more time after she mops, she's going to do something drastic or even kill him.

Grandpa then remembers he left his pretzels in the kitchen and goes back and dirties the floor again. Then sits back in the recliner putting dirty wet slippers in the air.

Granny gets her gun and without saying a word she shoots him dead in the recliner.

Granny calls 911 and tells them "I told my husband that if he walks through the kitchen after I mopped then I would kill him. He didn't listen and I shot him."

Emergency dispatch immediately sends an ambulance for Grandpa and a squad car for the wife. The Chief of Police hears about the call and thinks it's a rather strange story, so he drives to the house. When he gets there his officers are still waiting outside.

The Chief asks "Officers, What the hell! Why haven't you gone inside and arrested the woman?!"

"Sir we can't go in now. The kitchen floor is still wet."

Ever tried an Elvis Sandwich? Elvis would eat these PB&B sandwiches and there are variations and his mother, Gladys Presley said it was his favorite. [38]

The basic Elvis sandwich is peanut butter, crisp bacon and banana sandwich on toasted bread.

The bananas are sliced, and honey or jelly were sometimes added. Sometimes, Elvis preferred to have the bananas smashed. Then it would be put on toast or cooked in pan or griddle. [39]

Restaurants have been known to have this on their menus and Gladys, Elvis' mother, said he would eat several PB&B sandwiches.

News reports also mentioned Elvis ate the sandwich with caramelized bananas and crispy bacon on grilled Hawaiian bread, or grilled in bacon fat. [40]

Keeping up with the Joneses. Ever run into those who always one-up whatever you say? Do they ever boast about their BBQ unit?

Tell them to burn some money and buy the "Beefeater Gold-Plated Barbeque Grill" which only costs $164,000!

Made by a company based in Australia, this BBQ is nearly all 24-carat gold-plated, and they built it to create the "ultimate backyard status symbol." [41]   Except for the grilling surface, everything except the grilling surface is covered in 24-carat gold, and that includes the warming rack to the nuts and bolts.

The company estimated this gold-plated griller costs $164,000. The price may differ due to the fluctuating price of gold.

There's no melting since gold melts at around 2,000 degrees Fahrenheit and almost all grills max out at a mere 700 F.

Beefeater Gold-Plated Barbeque Grill

I love cooking with wine. "I love cooking with wine. Sometimes I even put it in the food."

-- W.C. Fields

National Cuisine. "Barbecue is the closest thing we have to a national cuisine.

"And Southern barbecue is the closest thing we have in the US to Europe's wines or cheeses. If you drive a hundred miles and the barbecue changes.

"Barbecue is the third rail of North Carolina politics."

- **John Shelton Reed,** American Sociologist

Cooking up some great snags isn't for the birds! True story. The kookaburra is an Australian native bird who was frequently given treats, bits of sausages and other BBQ meats from people barbequing in a Sydney park. The BBQ people would routinely toss treats to this particular kookaburra and these birds are meat eaters as they feed on mice or lizards in the wilderness.

The BBQ people were great cooks as the bird got very heavy and was overweight by almost one-half of its normal weight.

On one occasion, the bird was so heavy it couldn't fly, and dogs were chasing it. But a Sydney resident rescued the bird from the dogs and brought it to the Taronga Zoo in Sydney. where the wildlife nurse examined the bird and said, "Out in the wild she'd eat a whole small animal such as a mouse or skink (lizard), but butcher's sausages are just too much of a good thing," said Gemma Watkinson, Sydney's Taronga Zoo wildlife hospital nurse. [42]

"The kookaburra's been down at the rehabilitation aviary for a couple of weeks on a special 'lite n'easy' diet designed by our bird keeper," said the nurse. [43]

The zookeepers somehow got that bird committed to a steady exercise routine up to 3 times a day and it lost weight and eventually returned to the wild.

"We've styled the temporary home out like a 'bird gym'," the nurse reported. [44]

Keeping a level head. "If you are careful,' Garp wrote, 'if you use good ingredients, and you don't take any shortcuts, then you can usually cook something very good.

"Sometimes it is the only worthwhile product you can salvage from a day. What you make to eat.

"With writing, I find you can have all the right ingredients, give plenty of time and care, and still get nothing. Also true of love.

"Cooking, therefore, can keep a person who tries hard sane."

-- **John Irving**, excerpt from "The World According to Garp."

Self-deprecation. "I don't believe in degrading yourself into knots of excuses and explanations over the food you make.

"When one's hostess starts in with self-deprecations such as 'Oh, I don't know how to cook...,' or 'Poor little me...,' or 'This may taste awful...,' it is so dreadful to have to reassure her that everything is delicious and fine, whether it is or not.

"Besides, such admissions only draw attention to one's shortcomings (or self-perceived shortcomings), and make the other person think, 'Yes, you're right, this really is an awful meal! Maybe the cat has fallen into the stew, or the lettuce has frozen, or the cake has collapsed -- *eh bien, tant pis*!

"Usually, one's cooking is better than one thinks it is. And if the food is truly vile, as my ersatz eggs Florentine surely were, then the cook must simply grit her teeth and bear it with a smile -- and learn from her mistakes."

— **Julia Child, excerpt from "My Life in France."**

Caramel corn. "Anyone who thinks they're too grown up or too sophisticated to eat caramel corn, is not invited to my house for dinner."

— **Ruth Reichl**

What are the best fish for grilling?

Some suggestions. Salmon can withstand the heat of the BBQ and still maintains its taste.

Sword fish is available in stores and it's a firm meaty fish that is great to grill.

Tuna is very popular and tuna steaks medium rare seem to be a favorite with many people.

Snapper has a mild taste and great to grill and serve with asparagus, garlic BBQ baked potatoes, or pineapple for a tropical taste.

Red snapper, grouper, halibut are also great and hold their taste.

For expensive fish, probably the most expensive fish is the bluefin tuna to cook costing up to $5,000 per pound. These fish have a wide variety of fish in their diet and are almost circular in their diameter.

Anniversary riddle. A fancy restaurant in New York was offering a promotional deal. They advertised saying any married couple could eat at the restaurant for half-price on their anniversary.

Of course, the couple would need to bring proof of their wedding date.

But on one Thursday evening, a couple claimed it was their anniversary, but didn't bring any proof. The restaurant manager was called to speak with the couple. When the manager asked to hear about the wedding day, the wife replied with the following: "Oh, it was a wonderful Sunday afternoon, birds were chirping, and flowers were in full bloom." After nearly 10 minutes of ranting, she comes to tell him that today was their 28th wedding anniversary.

"How lovely", the manager said, "However, you do not qualify for the discount. Today is not your anniversary, you are a liar."

How did the manager know that it wasn't their anniversary?

Answer on p. 101

$$$$ Dessert. The most expensive dessert is "The Frrrozen Haute Chocolate Ice Cream Sundae" costing $25,000 which was added to the menu of the Serendipity 3 restaurant, New York, USA on 7 November 2007. [45]

Sound crazy? It is for real. The dessert uses a fine blend of 28 cocoas, including 14 of the world's most expensive. The sundae was made in partnership with luxury jeweler Euphoria New York.

The dessert is decorated with 5 g (0.17 oz) of edible 23-karat gold and is served in a goblet lined with edible gold. The base of the goblet is an 18-karat gold bracelet with 1 carat of white diamonds.

The dessert is eaten with a gold spoon, and the spoon itself is decorated with white and chocolate-colored diamonds, which can also be taken home.

Can you imagine everyone at your table saying, "Hey! I'll have one of those too!"

The previous record holder was called "The Serendipity Golden Opulence Sundae." It was much less expensive and only cost $1,000 and it held the record for three years, September 2004 until November 2007. [46]

Sandwich history. Going back to the 18th century, the sandwich that we are familiar with today started with John Montagu, 4th Earl of Sandwich, an eighteenth-century English aristocrat. [47]

He liked food presented to him like this since he loved to gamble and cribbage and other card games at public gambling houses for long hours.

If he was hungry, he would tell his valet to bring him salt beef between two pieces of toasted bread. He liked this since it allowed him to continue gambling while eating, without the need for a fork, and without getting his cards greasy from eating meat with his bare hands.

The dish then grew in popularity in London, and Sandwich's name became associated with it. [48]

It's like life itself. "Life Is like a big kitchen — you create, plan, organize, execute, achieve and sometimes you fail…"

— **Marcel Riemer,** "Slamming It Out! How I got sh*t done in 5 * kitchens"

BBQ. What's it worth? "No barbecue is worth anything unless it takes all day."

- **William Faulkner**

Some final thoughts on cooking.

"Real cooking is more about following your heart than following recipes. A recipe has no soul. You as the cook must bring soul to the recipe." – **Thomas Keller**

"Cooking is like painting or writing a song. Just as there are only so many notes or colors, there are only so many flavors—it's how you combine them that sets you apart." – **Wolfgang Puck**

"Cooking with kids is not just about ingredients, recipes, and cooking. It's about harnessing imagination, empowerment, and creativity." – **Guy Fieri**

"Cooking is at once child's play and adult joy. And cooking done with care is an act of love." – **Craig Claiborne**

"So, when people ask me, 'What do you think of Michelin?' I tell them I don't cook for guides. I cook for customers." – **Gordon Ramsay**

"Cooking is not difficult. Everyone has taste, even if they don't realize it. Even if you're not a great chef, there's nothing to stop you understanding the difference between what tastes good and what doesn't." – **Gerard Depardieu**

"Cooking requires confident guesswork and improvisation, experimentation and substitution. Also, it requires dealing with failure and uncertainty in a creative way." – **Paul Theroux**

"Cooking demands attention, patience, and above all, a respect for the gifts of the earth. It is a form of worship, a way of giving thanks." – **Judith B. Jones**

"Cooking demands attention, patience, and above all, a respect for the gifts of the earth. It is a form of worship, a way of giving thanks." – **Judith B. Jones**

"Food tastes better when you eat it with your family." -- **Anon.**

"When your intention is love, when you're doing something for people you love, it naturally turns out better. When you cook with love, even if you make mistakes, the food just tastes better. It's rather magical!" – **Mary Frances**

For the Greatest Cook Who Has It All!

Answers to Riddles

From p. 9 - What is it? Remove the outside, then cook the inside, then eat the outside, then throw away the inside. What is it?

A. Corn.

From p. 19 - If you had a pizza with crust thickness 'a' and radius square 'z', what's the volume of the pizza?

A. Volume is determined by pi times radius square times height. Or you could say,

*Pi times z squared times z times a or **Pi * z * z * a!***

From p. 24 - What did the grouchy baker make?

A. Crab cakes

From p. 44 - What did the astronaut cook in his skillet?

A. Unidentified frying objects!

99

From p. 54 - I get hot but hot, but I never sweat.

I cook things but I'm not a chef.

I have a door, but you don't go through me.

I can sometimes clean myself but I'm not a person.

I can be gas or electric but I'm not a car.

A. Oven

From p. 60 - What would a cake baked by a geologist be called?

A. Layer Cake

From p. 69 - You want to boil a two-minute egg. If you only have a three-minute timer (hourglass), a four-minute timer and a five-minute timer can you boil the egg for only two minutes?

A. Once the water is boiling, turn the three-minute timer and five-minute timer over. When the three-minute timer runs out, put the egg in the boiling water. When the five-minute timer runs out, two minutes have elapsed, and it is time take the egg out of the water. You don't need the four-minute timer for this riddle.

From p. 94 - Anniversary riddle. A fancy restaurant in New York was offering a promotional deal. A married couple could eat at the restaurant for half-price on their anniversary. To prevent scams, the couple would need proof of their wedding date. One Thursday evening, a couple claimed it was their anniversary, but didn't bring any proof. The restaurant manager was called to speak with the couple. When the manager asked to hear about the wedding day, the wife replied with the following: "Oh, it was a wonderful Sunday afternoon, birds were chirping, and flowers were in full bloom." After nearly 10 minutes of ranting, she comes to tell him that today was their 28th wedding anniversary.

"How lovely", the manager said, "However, you do not qualify for the discount. Today is not your anniversary, you are a liar."

How did the manager know that it wasn't their anniversary?

A. The calendar repeats itself every 28 years. So, if they were married on a Sunday 28 years ago, the day they were at the restaurant would also have to be a Sunday. Since it was a Thursday, the manager knew they were lying, and abruptly kicked them out of his restaurant.

We hope you enjoyed the book!

If you liked the book, we would sincerely appreciate your taking a few moments to leave a brief review.

Thank you again very much!

TeamGolfwell and Bruce Miller

Teamgolfwell.com

About the authors

Bruce Miller. Lawyer, businessman, world traveler, and author of over 50 books, a few being bestsellers, spends his days writing, studying, and constantly learning of the astounding, unexpected, and amazing events happening in the world today while exploring the brighter side of life. He is a member of Team Golfwell, Authors, and Publishers.

Team Golfwell are bestselling authors and founders of the very popular 340,000+ member Facebook Group "Golf Jokes and Stories." Their books have sold thousands of copies including several #1 bestsellers in Golf Coaching, Sports humor, and other categories.

We Want to Hear from You!

"There usually is a way to do things better and there is opportunity when you find it." - **Thomas Edison**

We love to hear your thoughts and suggestions on anything and please feel free to contact us at Bruce@TeamGolfwell.com

Other Books by Bruce Miller [49] and Team Golfwell [50]

Books in our "For People Who Have Everything Series (19 Books)" [51]

Brilliant Screen-Free Stuff to Do with Kids: A Handy Reference for Parents & Grandparents!

For the Golfer Who Has Everything: A Funny Golf Book

For a Great Fisherman Who Has Everything: A Funny Book for Fishermen

For a Tennis Player Who Has Everything: A Funny Tennis Book

The Funniest Quotations to Brighten Every Day: Brilliant, Inspiring, and Hilarious Thoughts from Great Minds

Jokes for Very Funny Kids (Ages 3 to 7): Funny Jokes, Riddles and More

Jokes for Very Funny Kids (Big & Little): Funny Jokes and Riddles Ages 9 - 12 and up and many more.

And many more…

Index

Looking good *1*

Kitchen truisms *1*

Outdoor cooking *3*

Who started to call it BBQ? *3*

Exhausting. *4*

Caring *4*

True story. *5*

Cutting the pizza. *6*

Cookies *6*

Does cooking food make us smarter? *6*

It's easy to make dinner... .... *7*

Loving food. *7*

A simple mistake *8*

What is it? *9*

Showing your love *9*

If your kids don't like milk. *9*

Think you're spending too much time in the kitchen? *10*

What it really is.. *10*

Gordon Ramsay *10*

Tough to clean the Microwave?............................ *13*

Question... *14*

Recipes... *14*

AI Chef... *14*

Low and Slow.... *17*

Homegrown.... *17*

If you're lookin', you're not cookin'....................... *18*

Cooking started millions of years ago *18*

Cooking Riddle. Determine Pizza volume *19*

Banned.. *19*

Veggies.... *19*

The truth comes out! *20*

No mistakes... *20*

Watermelon.. *20*

BBQ briskets slowly... *21*

Great BBQ *21*

Know how this feels *22*

What's for dinner? *23*

A Celebration! *23*

You don't mean that?! *23*

Not alone *23*

Cooking riddle. The grouchy baker *24*

BBQ? *24*

Cooking with wine *25*

Prepare the table and the guests too! *25*

I forgot my wallet! *25*

Why do men like to BBQ? *27*

Brits handle waiting in line (queue) well. W *28*

Try this on Movie Night – Popcorn Pizza! *28*

Kitchen sink *30*

Condiment pun *30*

Don't try Fugu at home! *31*

Marijuana in the BBQ *32*

The steaks have never been higher. *33*

Unusual pairing *33*

Grandma's cooking *33*

Pound cake *33*

Groaner *34*

Food to avoid *34*

Complicated cookbook *34*

Quick thinking *35*

A few observations about food *36*

Have you ever wondered why crackers have little holes? *37*

Cooking relieves stress *38*

Dolly's weakness *39*

Captions for Instagram pictures *39*

A $12,000 PIZZA! *41*

Tired of cooking in the kitchen? *43*

Great dinner Mom! *43*

Cooking Riddle. Outer space cooking *44*

Keep that BBQ brush handy! *44*

Condiments. " *45*

Air Fryer *46*

Ups and Downs of Air Frying *46*

Greasy situation – true story. *48*

An art form *49*

Fat-free frying. *49*

Like a woman *50*

The very first one. *50*

A few facts about flavor enhancers. *50*

Rodney may be exaggerating a bit. *52*

An old one about Bubba cooking a steak *52*

Two choices. *53*

Only an Australian Santa. *53*

The broken glass *54*

Kitchen riddle *54*

The Scotsman and his wife *54*

Leftovers? *55*

Senses *56*

That's a lot of beef? *57*

Let them fight it out *57*

Kitchen odors *57*

Original "Sh*t on a Shingle" *58*

Shortcut to good health. *60*

Strength. *60*

Groaner. *60*

Rocky cake riddle. *60*

Barbeque sauce. *61*

It's about others. *61*

Say again? *61*

Would you care for a few nuts and bee vomit? *62*

Two nuts. *62*

What everyone needs. *63*

Damn fish!. *63*

Leftovers. *64*

A special place *64*

Normal BBQ routine *65*

How you can tell? *66*

German Chocolate Cake *67*

Unusual sweet and salty combos *68*

Teach fishing *68*

Egg boil riddle. *69*

Cooking for life *69*

Whasamaddayou? *69*

Groaner *70*

Start of the Southern BBQ *70*

For what it's worth – a few unusual food facts *70*

Bad cooking *71*

What celebrities have said about food. *72*

How to cook Tigerfish *74*

Sauna steamed food *77*

Round ice cubes last longer than square ice cubes *78*

Hawaiian Pizza. *78*

Alligator *78*

A pancake story *79*

Wise words *79*

Woman in a restaurant. 79

Forced to eat 80

Downsides of cooking. 80

Loving food. 80

Transformer Decepticons 81

Choosing plates and palates 82

The art of cooking 82

Differences: Homemade pizza v. Restaurant pizza 82

Definition of "Hangry" 83

Unwritten cooking rules 83

Roof BBQ 84

I had a taste for kielbasa! 84

Facing the truth 85

"Old Hickory" 85

Love. 86

Don't mess with Granny 86

Ever tried an Elvis Sandwich? 88

Keeping up with the Joneses 88

I love cooking with wine *89*

National Cuisine *90*

Cooking up some great snags isn't for the birds! *90*

Keeping a level head. *91*

Self-deprecation *92*

Caramel corn *92*

What are the best fish for grilling? *92*

Anniversary riddle *94*

$$$$ Dessert *94*

Sandwich history *95*

It's like life itself *96*

BBQ. What's it worth? *96*

Some final thoughts on cooking *96*

Answers to Riddles *99*

Bruce Miller *103*

Team Golfwell *103*

References

---

[1] Barbecue, Wikipedia,
https://en.wikipedia.org/wiki/Barbecue

[2] Ibid.

[3] Taino, Wikipedia,
https://en.wikipedia.org/wiki/Ta%C3%ADno

[4] Ibid.

[5] "Invention of cooking drove evolution of the human species, new book argues: We are what we eat, and what we cook, The Harvard Gazette,
https://news.harvard.edu/gazette/story/2009/06/invention-of-cooking-drove-evolution-of-the-human-species-new-book-argues/

[6] Ibid.

[7] Ibid.

[8] "Our" food versus "my" food. Investigating the relation between childhood shared food practices and adult prosocial behavior in Belgium, Science Direct,
https://www.sciencedirect.com/science/article/abs/pii/S0195666314004656

[9] Ibid.

[10] BuzzFeed, AI Recipe generator,
https://www.buzzfeed.com/rossyoder/ai-recipe-generator

[11] Cooking, Wikipedia,
https://en.wikipedia.org/wiki/Cooking#:~:text=The%20oldest%20evidence%20(via%20heated,ago%20when%20hearths%20first%20appeared.

[12] Barbeque, Wikipedia,
https://en.wikipedia.org/wiki/Barbecue

[13] Ibid.

[14] Ibid.

[15] Most Expensive hamburger single portion, Guinness Book of World Records,

https://www.guinnessworldrecords.com/world-records/463544-most-expensive-hamburger-single-portion
[16] Fugu, Wikipedia, https://en.wikipedia.org/wiki/Fugu
[17] Young adults' use of food as a self-therapeutic intervention, The National Library of Medicine, https://www.ncbi.nlm.nih.gov/pmc/articles/PMC3991837/
[18] Ibid.
[19] Pizza, Wikipedia, https://en.wikipedia.org/wiki/Pizza#Records
[20] Ibid.
[21] "Man fights off sword-wielding attacker with a BBQ brush", Global News, https://globalnews.ca/news/1431110/watch-man-fights-off-sword-wielding-attacker-with-a-bbq-brush/
[22] Ibid.
[23] Ibid.
[24] "Do Air Fryers Have Health Benefits?", WebMD.com, https://www.webmd.com/food-recipes/air-fryers#:~:text=By%20most%
[25] Ibid.
[26] Federal Drug Administration report, Dept. of Health and Human Services, https://www.govinfo.gov/content/pkg/FR-1996-09-12/html/96-23159.htm
[27] Manuka honey, Wikipedia, https://en.wikipedia.org/wiki/M%C4%81nuka_honey
[28] Honey, Wikipedia, https://en.wikipedia.org/wiki/Honey
[29] Ibid.
[30] Obama Cuts In Line At Franklin Barbecue, Makes Up For It By Paying It Forward, HuffPost, https://www.huffpost.com/entry/obama-franklin-barbecue-pays-it-forward-austin_n_5577714
[31] Ibid.
[32] Tigerfish, Wikipedia, https://en.wikipedia.org/wiki/Tigerfish

[33] Food Psychology: How To Trick Your Palate Into A Tastier Meal, NPR, https://www.npr.org/sections/thesalt/2014/12/31/370397449/food-psychology-how-to-trick-your-palate-into-a-tastier-meal
[34] Ibid.
[35] Why does pizza taste so good, Colorado State University, https://source.colostate.edu/why-does-pizza-taste-so-good/#
[36] "Drunk man who wanted some sausages is jailed for arson after fire broke out when he started a barbecue in his sister's lounge", Daily Mail, https://www.dailymail.co.uk/news/article-2410951/Drunk-man-started-BBQ-living-room-booze-binge-wanted-sausages-jailed-arson.html
[37] Ibid.
[38] Peanut butter, banana and bacon sandwich, Wikipedia, https://en.wikipedia.org/wiki/Peanut_butter,_banana_and_bacon_sandwich
[39] Ibid.
[40] Ibid.
[41] "Check out the 10 most expensive BBQs in the World", Brian Pho, Luxatic, https://luxatic.com/check-out-the-10-most-expensive-bbq-grills-in-the-world/#google_vignette
[42] "Obese kookaburra given personal trainer", The Telegraph, https://www.telegraph.co.uk/news/newstopics/howaboutthat/7795793/Obese-kookaburra-given-personal-trainer.html
[43] Ibid.
[44] Ibid.
[45] Most expensive dessert, Guinness World Records, https://www.guinnessworldrecords.com/world-records/most-expensive-dessert#
[46] Ibid.
[47] Sandwich, Wikipedia, https://en.wikipedia.org/wiki/Sandwich
[48] Ibid.
[49] https://www.teamgolfwell.com/

[50] Ibid.
[51] Ibid.

Printed in Great Britain
by Amazon